# PASIFIKA NAVIGATORS

Pasifika Student Poetry Collection

# Pasifika Navigators Introduction

*A collaborative writing session with Malaga a le Pasefika class at Naenae College*

Pasifika ways of old and new
crash together.

A path where the right foot
can be the wrong foot.

Don't look left or right.
Look down at the moana.

Look up to the stars,
for we were once navigators.

Searching for new lands
in honour of old ones
always connected.

Descendants of
island warriors,
fierce and fearless,
moana crossroads and intersections
merge smoothly.

Time to awaken from your slumber,
rise to your feet Pasifika navigator

your va'a and your journey awaits,
set sail for your homecoming -
back to our ways
back to us,
back
to
You

# Mother Tongue

Tonight I will make sounds and form words
when put together, make sentences, make sense
        they say
I will speak in a language that is not mine, not ours,
        theirs.
It weighs down my brown tongue
colonizes my tone
civilizes my voice
a language I can't call my own.

This day like many other days
my mouth is torn between two trees
one rotting and the other growing
in New Zealand soil.
I am bold, brown and strong enough
but English has cut me up,
cut me down
made me forget the connection between my blood
and the soil of my motherland,
        Sāmoa.

I am forgetting.

Everyday
Mother
tells me, "a child owning two language is a smart child"
Uncle
tells me stories about our motherland and the war my ancestors
fought
shed blood
to redeem
to restore
to reclaim
        our mother tongue,
my beloved gagana.

And he does so in fa'asāmoa
I fear - where my poems will never reach.

Foolish
when I tell mother.
As if anyone could ever forget a language whose beauty
existence
cannot rely on the conversations I have with her.
As if my ancestors hadn't shed enough blood,
put their lives on the line for my brown tongue.
As if forgetting Samoan isn't forgetting a part of me
or our Atua who came before.

I am forgetting.

But
Mother still speaks to me in Samoan
even though my tongue is torn,
she speaks to me - to the other half
that I thought had died
buried
alive,
still deep within me.

Too stubborn to leave a tongue that fought so hard to survive?
No longer torn,
tongue finally ready to be one and pollinated with island seeds?
Maybe – my tongue isn't lost at all?
Could it be the history of my nation has woken me from my sleep?
The blood of my ancestors running through my veins?

Or is it the sadness that builds up inside my mother's eyes
when I say

"I am forgetting."

*Lili Williams, Year 12*

# Unity on the Battlefield

We enter the stadium fearless and proud.
The grass on this field is different from the homeland.
We walk on to see our opposition
a team of individuals.

We summon the Gods with our war cries -
Give us strength
Protect us
Let us be victorious.

Flying flags remind us of home,
hymns are sung echoing the voices of our ancestors.
Spirits filled
we have each other.

What is mistaken for islander competitiveness is survival of the fittest constantly tested.
The world of individuals wanting to bring us down.
They don't like our brown superpowers when united
their aim is to divide and conquer.

Our eyes meet.
We are not scared.
Tagaloa made us for battles like this.

Together we must remember who we are and to stay as one.
Fill our ears with our brothers, and sisters voices from the crowd.
Fill our hearts with the spirits of our mothers and fathers from our homes.

Drown out the taunting
criticism
hatred.
They just fear what they don't know.

But we know.

They will come for us with their words and we will get tackled.
Expect the unexpected because we will get back up.
They will try to make us believe we are not worthy
and we will run it straight
bursting through their lies.

They will try to make you forget who you really are -
but that's what makes us unstoppable.
Because we -
your team,
your 'āiga,
your ancestors
will never let you forget.

We are ready.
Whistle blows.

The game of our Polynesian lives.

*Olive Wip, Year 8*

# Aim Higher

the view she sees when standing in front of the mirror,
is not her reflection

Aim Higher

the goals she wants vs the goals they want,
she means no provocation

Aim Higher

not fitting in, not being them
doesn't mean she doesn't want to be a part of the constellation

Aim Higher

looking around wanting the Pālagi world to walk a day in her
brown shoes just to feel some type of connection

Aim Higher

she studies hard, gives it her all, and yet she still feels out of reach

Aim Higher

her struggles, she cannot verbalise or comprehend
she can no longer handle the heat

Aim Higher

she loses focus, she gets distracted
she stumbles on her brown plantation feet

Aim Higher

she knows it's a trap, where we never win
and no longer wants to compete

## Aim Higher

trying her best to be at the top of her class,
no matter what she does always an outcast

Aim Higher.

she is just a Samoan-Niuean girl
who no longer wants to be a part of this Pālagi Empire
and through all her trials and tribulations,
all she hears in the echo of her mind, her heart and soul is

Aim Higher

*Nyssa Ng-Lam, Year 13*

# No mistakes, No problems

Sau i!
Heavy legs
Heart pounds
Blood pumping
Mind numb
World slows
Their faces
Laughter in the background
Nana minding her own business
My face
Red with anger
Wet salty face
His Face
"Sau ku i!"
Don't look up
Tear drops hitting the hard carpet
Vision goes blurry
Eyes red
Watch your mouth
Watch your eyes
Heart skipping beats
Scared and distressed
Protective shield ready
Aua le kaukilaikiki
No accidents
No mistakes
No tears allowed
No, No, No
Live, ~~love~~, learn

*Fereni Laki, Year 9*

# An Island

my origins
just sand and ocean
an island.
Family tell me
I am also blood and bones.

I try and define the sand
there laid the soil.
I look for blood,
there was the sea.

Tinau said, "Connect to the deep sea."

I close my eyes and imagine
that the malicious and unwavering sea gave me sight of unending
battles of the ocean
suffocating an island

securing a grip of risk in a future
that is met with only devastation and loss
drowning precious lands

so then I knew, there were to be of a shatter in this culture
binds that were once held sacredly and heartily.

But now being torn to bits of invisible struggles.

Struggles that are overlooked by a big world
known as a country sinking, only to some.

But is so special to a small group of people
an ancestral land that dug many ancestors
who are now considered the old, a past.

But built this culture
from afar where I can call the unseen
An unknown country, I name home ...
Kiribati.

Now a culture who seemingly
inhale and mimic the silver life of the Pākeha
with no kinds of sticks or stones
travelling from a breaching island and building up ties
in a birthplace of concrete and leather
giving birth under their silver lights
and maybe hoping to be fed with a silver spoon.

Fed in a tsunami of influence washing out our tongues
from our motherland
so there again, my imagination shows me
the same depiction of the mighty sea who lurks.
I begin to countlessly see a taunting vision of my home sunk
within the depths of the heavy ocean.

So when our lands are finally in the grasp of climate change
and its ruthless rising.
Where will the upcoming generations of our bloodline be raised?
Will there be no more of the gilbertese?
Is there only blood and bones now?
No more of the sand and peaceful ocean,
but now a soil where a new sprout is to begin.

Forgetting its roots
bathing in flavourless rain and raised by a blind sun.

Our blood overtaken by predictions
that we would be of no more in just above forty years as a country
with a great impact of diversity withering a future generation.
Now, I open my eyes, attentive
and look to my generation.

That my people,
now chase the stars
but the old, now a shaded moon.
My people now love the rivers
but the old has become the ocean.
My people now hum of inconsistency
but the old, will always hum rhythmically

*T.M., Year 12*

# ‘Uliuli sheep

Skin judged
fa‘asinomaga changed
too brown for white
too white for brown
never acknowledged
always told.

Tagi, tagi. tagi
at words that fill my ears
the hate that would be inflicted on me
just because of my lanu.

Unknown to my mātua,
my lagona
so I kept it like that.
I fesiligia my identity and colour
told I couldn’t be Samoan
la‘ulu too straight
mata too chingy.

No one likes different

I know.

*Jeilah Afamasaga, Year 7*

# Grandma & Nana

Grandma speak Tongan to me
Samoan to me
wanting to learn it
guessing game
odd one out
secret code
point and
say in Tongan
always happy
us being around her
tough love
you fat - ke fu'u sino!
every Sunday
time with her
hold our hands
looking forward
to seeing us
Tongan music
from the tv
pull hair –
rats tail
cut it off!
first to come
strong
loving
hugs and
armwrestles

no more
Sunday visits
different life
holding her hands
grandma sideline support
we miss you
you are here and
we will look after our sister
look after each other
we know that you
are at peace
love, loss and healing
when we think of
Grandma

Nana always talk to us
do good in school
stay in school
never fight
Cook Island
Tongan
broken English
Funny joker
hard worker
always cleaning
slept anywhere
ate with hands
six children
still pick us up
after school
take us
to her work
quiet
chill
caring
Cooking
giving
loving
doughnuts
for sale

now gone
up above
different love
no more
proud smiles waiting
we love you
we will be okay
because you taught us
to listen to our parents
no more pain
sadly happy
for you to keep guiding us
your heartbeats
Nana

*Logan Woolley, Year 10*

# Being Tongan

Tongan traditions
family, hierarchy and status
outstanding feats

always climbing
coconut palms and hunting with spears
no shoes needed

ta'ovala on
gathering glorious crabs, fish from the moana
village leader setting up tables for everyone to eat
mountain horizons
clear reflections of the blue heavens

responsibility
to family
to sisters
to mother

coming together
sharing prayers
staying together

'Ale is my connection to my ancestors
is everything to me.

Church celebrations
birthday feasts
assigned tables and seats

Ideas - building, creating, umu
food rewards
yummy kasava, taro, kumara, 'otai, tusipi
and the most amazing potato salad.

Tongan and English
Kindness is important
Respect above everything

*Katiloka ʻAle, Year 7*

# Expect the Unexpected

Expectations grow as you grow older

Expectations haunt as they get harder

Expectations of the only girl means high beam on

Expectations to automatically know what to do
    without being told

Expectations of the youngest are not as easy as they say

Expectations of the last one in school carrying failed siblings
dreams along the way

Expectations of a different story or path to follow

Expectations where you are always someone's role model

Expectations of making your parents, grandparents,
    and village proud

Expectations so high you will think you are in the longest
    marathon of your life

Expectations of a minister's daughter are near impossible

Expectations around never making mistakes and to always use
    your māfaufau

Expectations of a life with hidings and lectures

Expectations to do better than good at school

Expectations to walk, talk, sit and smile right

Expectations of never having freedom to breathe

Expectations of having no one to talk to about what you're
    going through

Expectations of being here on earth longer than you want to be

Expectations of leaving and no one knowing

Expectations for talking to the man above every night

Expectations that He gives me comfort and a break
from my thoughts

Expectations that He gives me more than a reason to still be here

Expectations that He helps me to see the beauty in my life

Expectations to learn that nothing is impossible

Expectations that even storms run out of rain

*Netaa Misa S, Year 11*

# Laugutu

My Grandma's name.
My name
your mouth
your words
cut deep.

Like ...
"Polys are scary"
"Coconuts"
"Big nose"
"Big feet"
"Big frizzy hair"
"Dark skinned people are good black slaves."

Still human
with feelings.

Like...
Ashamed
Frustrated
Tired
Sad
Angry.
You don't see us,
who we really are.

Like ...
Humble hard workers
The human form of alofa
Serving and giving
Proud Pasfika warriors
Natural born navigators
God fearing people
You fear what you don't know

Can't say, see or feel like
US
then "Va'ai lou gutu ..."
my Grandma's favourite saying

Watch your mouth.

*Siobhan Sa'u, Year 7*

# Our Power

Native women ignored.
Positioned to speak of testimony
contrasts leaving women voiceless.
Collections of dark history. Colonial power images the female body.
Identity
and
society.

Painting the gaze of indigenious bodies.
Living on the spectrum.
Outspoken,
then silenced.
Breaking politics at its centre.
Reinscribing women by episode.
A symbol of a boat that collapsed.
Double-voiced of romance.
A mutiny device that colonised women.
No diversity but Polynesian beauty
Attacks addressed an object.
A PI woman.
Truth
masks
our
voices.
A culture deconstructed in history.
Western desire advertising power.

"I'm where we once belonged" presents the Pālagis' continued work to cover the interest of status,

past

and

present.

Our power, as silent like the whispers of the lullabye tune of my mother's voice.

"You strip me bare," they said.
"You strip me bare," I say.

*Cedar Porteous, Year 13*

# ʻāiga is

Everything to me
my respect and effort
No. Matter. What.
Family first.
Different ways like love, kindness, respect.
Respect faʻasāmoa and ʻāiga.
Respect your parents and elders.
Say Tūlou, excuse me.
You do what they ask of you.
They have wisdom.
They know what is right.

Gather in the lounge
prayers of gratitude.
We harmonize not just in song
but In Life.
Everyone has their parts
Jobs, roles, duties to fulfil.
We talanoa.
How is everything going?
What has everyone done in the day?
We laugh and love.
We share stories.

Let the elders eat first,
Uma? finished?
Get them an ʻapa and towel
for them to wash and dry their hands.
Then take their plates back -
for the many plates they filled with food to fill your belly
while they sacrificed and went hungry.
Feaus or chores
every morning

every day
wake up and clean.
A new day is a new chance
to serve, to give back
and make my ‘āiga proud.

Sunday morning church
helping Mum with the to‘ona‘i
wearing white.
We all stand in rows and look the same
everyone knows everyone.
We are a village.
We learn lessons from Jesus
always together.
Feeling blessed.
Go home
back to the start.

We are one
If one has a problem
we all have a problem.
Never alone,
always someone
somewhere
some person to go to.
Vā
bonds us and keeps us -
connected
through alofa, tautua, and fa‘aaloalo
through love, service, and respect.

This is ‘āiga, and my ‘āiga
is my Everything.

*Cialla Loto, Year 8*

# What do you see?

Tell me why you don't expect people like me to succeed
from our skin as dark as the trunks of the trees
to our loud, proud and profound personalities -
What do you see?

Do you see young educated minds of the Pacific
or angry, unbothered kids who are 'illiterate'
with both parents who do not share your mother tongue
that automatically gives you the right to make fun.
My ancestors voyaged across the seven seas
with only the guide of the stars and the soft, cool breeze
and yet, you have the audacity
to look down on me?
Because back in the islands we relied on our families
to work, harvest, grow and collect what we need
without the help of technology
yet you insist that your way
is the only way to succeed -
What do you see?

Tell me why you don't expect people like me to be free
is it because we do not share the same priorities?
Family, Church and School
I did not have the same upbringing as you
at dawn, the women sing to thank the Lord for a new day
and the little children gather around them to pray -
What do you see?

Doctors, Dentists, Lawyers, in your eyes are out of our reach
because in class 'we're difficult to teach'
Entrepreneurs, CEOs, Engineers, is out of our grasp
because in the 'real world'
white people have the power
Rugby Players, Tradies and Cleaners to you
is all we'll ever be
because my people are incapable of obtaining any degree
of success according to you -
What do you see?

Tell me why you don't understand who we are
from the honour and privilege of our tatau
intricate designs forever permanent on our bodies
showing the line between youth and maturity
telling our story ...
From the power and strength of our chee-hoos
calling out to Malietoa
you hear us before you see us, but do you really see us?
Do you really hear us?
You think it is very rare for us to achieve so big
and when we do you become so blue
that your mind cannot comprehend it and it mustn't be true
because we have not done it like you -
What do you see?

From the bold and fierce pukanas of our Māori,
warrior brothers and sisters
to the maturity and wisdom shining from the gold smiles of our
Tongan brothers
to the heart racing meke of our Fijian cousins
to the beautiful, 'ei katu crowns that adorn the heads of our
Cook Island neighbours
to the musical talents of our Tokelauan kāiga
for our myths and legends, are true indeed
the mana of our ancestors that planted the seed
for future generations to inherit and lead - What do you see?

My people, woman or man, young or old
rising as Kings and Queens
like in the stories foretold
continue to be loud, proud and bold
for our futures, worth and dreams cannot be controlled.
For we were taught to never go down without a fight
and instead spread our wings, be bold and take flight
in a society that wants to keep us quiet
we will continue to express ourselves and defy it
for the same stars that guided my ancestors across the seas
are the same stars that will guide us to the success of our dreams.
I know what I see.

*Beka Sa'u, Year 13*

# White

White
the colour of my skin.
But
brown eyes.
White with brown smarts
but I love faiteles.
White like my family expectations
but I embrace fa'asāmoa.
White with straight Pālagi hair
but at the back of the siva.
White and eat povi
but I cook sapa sui.

I have culture
I have culture
I have culture.

When will you accept me?
Will you hear me?
You see me?

Brown eyes.
But
feeling the colour of my skin ...

... invisible

*Denzil Perez, Year 9*

# Tusitala.

Tusitala
Who sounded the tales of the tides
Tusitala
Who rests atop a giant,
Surrounded by the blooming teuila and fading oriana
Forever honoured in the eyes of the heavens

Tusitala
Who drew influence from the ground
Drew the faces of the people:
"Little Indian, Sioux, or Crow,
Little frosty Eskimo,
Little Turk or Japanese,
Oh! don't you wish that you were me?"
Tusitala
Forever a 'Top 10 must see in Sāmoa'

Tusitala
Who crawled among us
Wove his web with derogatory terms and harmless words:
"Such a life is very fine,
But it's not so nice as mine:"

Built mansions on our plantations
Destroyed our natural resources with his importations
Made a profit off our pain
Desecrated the natural plains

Tusitala
The writer who 'blessed' our lands with fame
Formed our alienation
Replaced our oceans with fountains
And still rests
Atop the mountain.

*Oriana Ewens, Year 12*

# Always

be proud
of who you are and where you are from
don't forget to always embrace your culture.

Always
when performing
"Ata ata mai"
when praying
"Tatou ifo ma tatalo"
put God at the forefront of your life.

Always
show respect to your elders
Fa'avae Sāmoa i le Atua - God is our foundation
remember your family is with you.

Always
Do your best
Be your best
in everything you do
because you will always belong to us.

In all your Pasifika ways
fa'avavau, fa'avavau lava.
Always.

*Eliana Paara Taula, Year 8*

# Never Again

enter the room with shadow overhead
shame and embarrassment are my real shadow,
fear of them opening their mouths.
Island human label for an island girl like me,
stressed at the thought of another butchered attempt

correct them, teach them they say
'It's who you are', she whispers.
Nana is right.
My queen sits proudly on the throne in my mind
giving me strength to break through
the fear
the teasing
the giggles
that paralyses me.

Today, my queen has fallen
off her throne
nowhere to be felt.
I see white mouths moving,
hear white sounds.
I am used to white apologies
where nothing changes.
And just when I feel my island spirit taking its last breath
my queen grabs hold of me
pulls me close to say,

'Never again'

*Vaina Hunt, Year 13*

# My fa'amalu

Protector and shield from the storms
meaningful traditions
kept alive by the island blood under skin
culturally strong

A new door to womanhood and identity
delicately painful
patterns depicting pride and stories of long ago

Inked duties of service that keep me clothed
pains for Sāmoa

My home
My country
My heart

For I have been chosen
to receive this gift from the heavens

alofa mai
alofa atu

*Nikolah Teofilo, Year 8*

# Real learning

From island beginnings
i miss home.

Moved to the bright lights
Overwhelming.

Don't remember
Changing.

New Pālagi world
Different.

Change the way i move, look and sit
Stressful.

Not just english, but Good English
Pressure.

Being the bridge between worlds for my family
Lost.

Always shape shifting and expected to be strong
Balancing everything.

Feeling Stupid everyday
I am from other islands across the Pacific too.

No one cares
There are no credits attached.

Not worth it

Need more assignments on acceptance.

Or about real life for us

You say the words.

No actions

What I see and feel.

What is happening to me

Is real life.

Real learning

...

*Faimafili Sa'e Tasi, Year 9*

# The art of change

Pulefou. Vailima. Sugashi. Pritchard.

Born, 2003 March 28, a fighter

Named after two great men who helped my Family,

two seas crossed to name a force of nature

My Kiega was the gateway to my feminine

My Kama was the type of man that leaves a chocolate under your pillow
every night,
for every morning

My siblings are my giants
*they,*
be my protectors on the hardest days

Sutton Park, Manurewa East School, St Joseph's
through the cracks we resided
all the single kieges

It took a village to raise the Beyoncé in my Family

This one's for the Laura's,
The Eddie's,
The Jay's,
The Fonosisi's

For the women that protected me fiercely Lexiga,
Tyler,
Linda,
Juliette

Thank you

In our society

When you present as male

you are expected to be an alpha within the pack

We sign away your emotions

You sign a pact.
To never cry, publicly

To speak mostly when spoken to

To be one of the boys

To choose wisely when revealing how you feel

Mask it with anything but gay

To be a man you have to act like a man, walk like a man

if you cry out your a poof-ta
What echoes back is
they don't know what to do with their emotions, most times

But somethings just can't disappear

Pray the gay away, New Zealand

What hits back is that violence isn't always an answer

To survive, The boys I know learned what other people told them
The boys i know
Would kick a bin to prove their manly,
assert their masculinity,
rather than shed a tear drop

We build our men to break

Tell them to express their emotions

Yet demonise a man's tears

Their taught to be afraid of fragile

Paint insults on bodies they understand

So,
To those who weren't ashamed to be seen with me
To Gabriel the baddest Philippino I know,
to both the Noahs, to Mafi Minaj
Thank you

When you present as male

You have to ***choose*** the women you will become

This one's for the Jaycee's, the Akasha's, The Fangs
This one's for Moe,
always know you'll be the Mistress Supreme

I've crossed the margins in the textbook,
a place where only a few dare to go.

I dream the day everyone will say my name

Truth is I've been avoiding this poem because of how real it is

I've struggled being pushed out

Home hasn't always felt like home

But this body, this body will always be my first

Love it no matter what

I am Pasifika Trans woman

Brave, beautiful, and bold

No matter what anyone says I'll whisper

I love myself

Till it's the loudest in the Universe, till my name

Stellar Aigagalefili Makarita Pritchard

Is no longer a question

To go from that boy, this woman, this Queen,
who in this very  is slaying her Goliath with a sling,
who in this very moment made peace with all her demons,

Who in this very moment feels....

Loved

Thank you

*Stellar Pritchard, Year 13*

# If Pasifika was a person

Pasifika would help me learn more about my culture
and the history behind it.
Pasifika would be a massive part of my life,
who I am
and where I come from.
Pasifika would tell us stories what it was like
growing up in the islands -
our ancestors
Tagaloa and our toa warriors.
Pasifika would show the world our power
to always get back up
to never give up
to change the world for the better.
Pasifika would teach us about respect
love
and how to serve
eachother.
Pasifika would remind me to be proud
of who I am
when the world tells me otherwise.
Pasifika would be a mirror showing me who I really am
where I have come from
and who I am destined to be.

*A.J. Papalii, Year 8*

# Roots

Ideas, thoughts whispered in my head.
Cookies
loud and bright standing out
long straight hair
not mine.
Tight bushy curls obstructing my vision
makabush
mocking friends.
Me and my culture the target
big feet
drink and party
everything is chill.
Too chill.

Another coconut from a different coconut tree bunga.
Jokes not funny.
Raro, not the sugary drink
but my skin is an illusion
not what you think.

Challenge what you see
found in tīvaevae
seen in our tiare
An ‘ei katu crown sits on my proud island curls.
Island beauty on the inside and out.
Dancing,
beautiful drumming.
guitar.

My roots ground me
quieten the world.
Focus on the moana
let the Cook Island soil bring me home.
My heaven on earth.

*Maia Fergusson, Year 7*

# Freedom

Freedom
choosing what I want
"I don't know" doesn't mean I won't know
money is not my incentive
status is not success
island spirit under attack

| Pulling | Pushing |
|---|---|
| Be this! | Be that! |
| All for you? | Where am i? |
| Who am i? | Do you care? |

I am drowning in your dreams for me.

I wait for the day to choose
act        say        what I want
... for me

Please
school system take your foot off my neck
let me breath
I just need a taste of freedom
to keep
my head
my body
above ground
world let me be

let me breathe

*Carmen T, Year 13*

# My Fiji

Grains of sand fall through my fingers
Hot humid breeze carries the sound of the ocean waves to shore
Fijian smiles hypnotize
Happy bare feet as we take a drink from the fresh coconut juice

Oh so sweet.

Turtles gather and paddle on by
Friendly neighbours
Everything is part of the circle of Fijian life
The coral keep secrets that only the stingrays know
Looking up at the sky and wonder how heaven landed
on our shores

Sun sets and a glowing moon rises with the stars
welcoming our ancestors.

A story re-told when you hear the lali in the distance
Fearless Fijian fire walkers and warriors light up the dark skies
Our strength from our home land
Carried by our spirits to new lands

Vinaka Fiji.

*Aryan Pathak, Year 8*

# Dear Little Brown kid

Little Brown kid

**You. Are. Enough.**
When the education system says otherwise
**You** Are Enough.
When your culture isn't valued in the space
You **Are** Enough.
And when they don't give you the time, the energy and the love
that you deserve.
Little brown kid you better shut that voice up in your head because
You. Are. **Enough.**

**Ancestral patterns Etched on Taupou skin**
Where do I begin?
In order to win we must look within.

Throwback Thursday -
They called us Savage but our systems were sacred
Stories silenced by the storm of salivating sailors in the sea,
Who **violated our women, our land**
but now I take the stand
To speak on behalf of my ancestors **whose mouths were sewn shut**
but their screams forever echo through generations.

"Koe mahu'inga ae ako, koe teuteu kihe kaha'u aho'o mo'ui."
The purpose of school is to build a foundation for your future.
But what if school isn't our safe space?

Teachers force us to believe, that in order to succeed
We need to concede and earn our degrees.

But when my brown brothers bleed in these streets
I have no choice but to work and feed
The mouths of these other brown kids
So that degree seems worthless to me.
When push comes to shove,
Labels start speaking

They say 'Your mental health comes later, you can't do any better'
**All this because I wear a warehouse sweater**
**Instead of the $80 school jacket you pressure me to wear.**

It's a fair race they say:
**But why is every path blocked with signs saying 'road works ahead'...**
ironic because the road wouldn't even work if Uncle Sione wasn't working there.

Now here comes John from AGGS:
***Privilege* prancing passionately across the pavement.**
**Yes, that still exists. Class division still exists.**
**You see, these badges might be from central but my brain is from Nuku 'Alofa.**
While me and my girls tangutu at the back of class,
We remind ourselves, they're only assigned seats not assigned roles
**But being classically underserved continuously,**
**discrimination feels like it's chillaxing with us permanently.**
**Longo.**
There's silence while we watch this stereotypical cycle repeat again and again

**And then ... they have the nerve to tell us who we are, where we come from and what we need to learn in order to succeed? The audacity!**

Forcing languages down our throats like a bad packet of throaties.
I don't need no French or Latin; I can speak my own language.
No - I don't need to re quote Shakespeare,
**I am a descendant of ancestors who been telling stories**
**since the dawn of creation.**
**So save it!**

Because while your ancestors were busy building systems of racism & colonisation
my ancestors were traversing the largest ocean in the world.

Stop trying to rewrite our story
Stop trying to 'understand'
Stop trying to compare
Cause we've had enough
and we'll tell our own story, thanks.

I know I sound angry, and yeah I am.
But I also know that there's hope at the end of a dark tunnel.
Teutalanome vahe 31, veesi 6
he ko Sihova ko ho 'Otua ko ia ia 'oku hā'ele mo kimoutolu;
'e 'ikai tene fakatukuhāusia'i koe, 'uma'ā ha'ane li'aki.

Little brown kid

Remind yourself everyday that you **descend from greatness and you belong to the generation of change.**
Become the bigger person your ancestors fought for you to be, for we are **the game changers, the rule breakers, the mistake makers, the mountain shakers, the earth quakers.**
**And it is an honour to be Polynesian.**

Little brown kid - keep your head up high
Because at the end of the day
You. Are. More than. Enough.

*Eniselini Ali, Year 12*

# My Name is Ofa

They turn and laugh
shrinking as my culture is stripped from my soul.

Teacher calls on me
the Pālagi me
to just accept her efforts
and give in.

Saddened and ashamed
nothing new.
Only the new normal.
Society sucks
at least this one.
Must fit into their name narrative.

No thought.

No effort.
No need.
Disney-level entry snow-girl?

NO!

Say it properly.
Spell it correctly.
Roll call gone wrong.
It all continues.

Don't you know it means love.

I am made from love
but get no name love.
My Nana's namesake
gone before I was born and watching on from above
waiting for change
like me ...

*Ofa Alataua, Year 7*

# I Wish

Afro
Papuan dimdim
light skin.

"Honest, but you don't look like that?"
Look like one to be one?
Big, puffy, curly, frizzy.

No wig
touching and pulling
hurting
me.

It's real
left out
Look out
Out of control.

Tied up
untameable
too tight
too knotty.

Frizzy
hide it
cut it off
shave it off.

Come back prettier, smoother, softer
dreaming
wanting
wishing.
For none of it.

Only
acceptance.
of my papuan hair,
of me.

*Navili Maladina, Year 10*

# Samoan Siapo

Small brown strips
gifts from the tree
Water stretched and beaten
Sounds echo across the fanua
tap, tap, tap
Sharp edged, scraping paua

Grandma
surrounded
by old women
surrounded by tautua
surrounded by alofa
together

Bark made flat and smooth
Light brown sheet
hanging to dry
warm Samoan air
singing
smiling
working
gifting

She is my ‘āiga,
She is my fatu.

*Christian Faitotoa Alualu Lualua, Year 8*

# Atua

I ask myself what my Samoan ancestors would think
I don't mean about me attending church
because in fact
fa'asāmoa is founded on God
and encourages the church
and advocates for the faith.
So what happened to Tagaloa?

Rather, I wonder what they think about
the name 'England' being connected to my Anglican church,
England,

the heart of colonization.
            Sāmoa,
the heart of Polynesia and victims of colonization.

Why didn't Tagaloa fight for us?

Some may say to leave history behind
to simply move on and forget.
But what do they say to a colonised Samoan descendent
whose colonisers' blade has left its rust stains?
Blood that cannot dissolve
cannot be eliminated in me.

But could have eliminated Tagaloa?

Brainwashed to believe that the colonizers
that once killed, once took, once stole
were okay to cleanse and bring forth the word of God.
Lacking consultation with ancestors,
compassion for mātua,
alofa towards tamaiti.

Leading us to believe that their God is mightier than our Tagaloa?

I'm therefore split
between the foundation on which my ancestors stood upon -
first Tagaloa and now the colonizer's God,
and how my ancestors saw their ʻāiga killed by the blades of our God's own colonizers.
Questions - is God white? Is God brown?
Confusion. Cultural conflict.
And I can't help but ask,

"What would Tagaloa do?"

*Sharlene Viliamu-Letalu, Year 13*

# Tropical blend

I am a tropical blend
Tālofa lava. I am Samoan.
Mālō e lelei. I am Tongan.
Fakalofa lahi atu. I am Niuean.
Confused where to start,
becoming the person everyone wants.
What do I really want?
Being prayed over.
Afraid of disappointment.
Make your family proud.
Grandpa's from Savaii.
Make your family proud.
Nana is from Tamakautoga.
Make your family proud.
Mum is from Vaimalo.
Make your family proud.
Dad is from Ma'ufanga.
I am a tropical blend.

*Amelia Kerisiano, Year 10*

# ‘Ie lāvalava

‘Ie lāvalava strapped tight to my waist
like a seatbelt for my safety
society proves the motive for this matter.
Worn for traditions.

Expressions of identity and culture
knotted tightly to help me remember.
Worn for respect.

Modesty is the rule with nothing to bare
sitting covered crossed legged
‘ie lāvalava the shield.
Worn to protect.

Watching boys’ legs breathing freely
while mine are caged in cloth
overprotectiveness unnecessary.
Worn for traditions.

Topless ancestors and grass skirts
all before missionaries covered us up.
Worn for respect.

Given the chance mine would be styled
three quarter, mini skirt or shorts even
protecting my innocence is not an option
unless I shy away from all this corruption.
Worn to protect.

But dad says that's the Pālagi way
where they think showing less is more
fathers, brothers live their lives/life freely
while the heart of the family constantly lives restlessly
stay on the straight and narrow path
cover your sacred God-given flesh.
Worn for traditions.
Worn for respect.
Worn to protect.

Or face the wrath of islander disgust
and a first class ticket to hell.

*Monica Ng-lam, Year 13*

# Puzzle Pieces

Remember the box with different shaped holes and
puzzle pieces that fit?
The goal was to match the correct shape with the correct hole.
Innocent little hands clumsily fumbled with the pieces.
Trying to shove the star into the square hole at the top of the box.

> I am the star puzzle piece.
> My life is the box.
> Those hands are mine.
> Does it fit? Do I fit in?

I'm not a fully white or brown star.
My five corners pointing in all directions trying to escape people
who are speaking an unknown language.
Have you ever seen a star that doesn't shine?
Embarrassed and nervous at the stares waiting for me to shine like
the Pacific Island sun I was born under.
The moon waits for me to reply, expecting me to talk.
But it's easy when the moon knows what it is and its job.
My cheeks and ears burn up.
Wishing the pitch black night would just open up and swallow me.

> I am the star puzzle piece.
> My life is the box.
> Those hands are mine.
> Does it fit?    Do I fit?

*Jet Vailini, Year 8*

# Owning Me

stranger to my own culture
on the outside always looking in
not understanding how things are done
no teachings to guide or hold my hand
getting put to work, doing nothing right
not knowing why, I just look and listen
unable to communicate with'āiga from the mainland
I never knew we lived in villages
expected to know everything
as if God had pre-programmed us
just coz I'm Samoan in a foreign country
surrounded by different people
some the same, it's still different.

Questioning - Am I really Samoan?
searching for answers
talking to the knowledgeable
learning to understand
feeling courageous
wanting to know more
needing to know more
          because I am more.

Using all the knowledge
Gathering the confidence to own that part of me.
    Expressing the culture through siva.
    Learning the language.
    Speaking the language.
    Singing the songs in which my ancestors did before me.
    Visiting and standing on the very soil
    where my bloodline started
    Experiencing what it's like to be a part of a village.

Finally feeling brave enough, proud enough to say
    "I am Samoan"

*Geordina Togia, Year 11*

# My string

there is a string
it's tied
keeps me safe
whole.
my polynesian circle
where I belong.

I am a Māori
but
I'm curious
about what my other culture holds in store for me.
I learn and learn
like a seed waiting to bloom
but suddenly -
clouds block the sun
stops me from growing.

They shut the gates
keeping my culture at a distance
the string tightens
part of me taken away.

Getting harder
the world pulls at my string
wants to break in
keep me disconnected
afraid of losing it forever.
I am taught what I already know.
deprived.

My culture.
My language.
My identity.
now in the centre of the string
an empty void
trying to keep the string connected
holding on
arms stretched out
must reach the other side to keep together
Struggling.
Snap.
Broken.

Please help me fix my string.

*B.Hine, Year 9*

# Islands in the stream

Islands don't belong in streams.
Shallow water cannot help islands grow or be understood.

Racist undercurrents hold it in place.
Stuck between rocks,
scrapping the bottom along the way
this island is destined to fail.
With the dream of flourishing coconut trees
NOT ACHIEVED.
Culture and identity stripped bare
to be like the stream controllers,
Gatekeepers.

No leaders needed.
Isolated.
Lonely.
Dying
islands.

But I've seen islands in the moana.

Flourishing in the light of
Connections,
Unity.
Commanding tidal waves.
Powered by language and acceptance.
These islands only see
MERIT and EXCELLENCE upon the horizon.
Anchored in diversity
and endless opportunities.
Powered by journeying together.
Opportunities along the moana are endless.

Inter-connected.
Learning.
Living.
Thriving.
Achieving.

Streams resist the moana's power,
but with help from the almighty -
His winds, waves, and currents built upon
Hope.
Faith.
Dreams.
That help us dismantle restricted streams that trickle
into the darkness of shallow puddles

No more tomorrow,
or on the soon to never come list
It was yesterday for the generations of my people who drowned.
It is now for my people today to fulfil their destinies by
commanding the moana,
because the day has come
where all streams flow freely,
where WE flow freely into the moana -

Where we belong.

*Mercy Ili, Year 13*

# Fa‘aaloalo

Foundation of my being
taught to me from birth.
Through listening, watching and doing.
A duty to serve with alofa
and out of gratitude.
A core value of the Samoan Culture
at my core.

Respect for my grandparents.
Appreciation
for the sacrifices they made
coming to the land of milk & honey
leaving their home
all they knew behind.
For me.

Respect for my parents.
For doing what they have to
for the time they are away.
Working hard to provide for us
giving us all the things they did not have
growing up.
Now grown.

Respect for myself.
Knowing me
seeing me for me.
Mirror for my parents
my younger siblings
and the world around me.
I am an afakasi princess
blessed and proud.
Born to a Samoan King & Kuki Airani Queen.

*Elise Taula, Year 8*

# old home, new world

Sāmoa
Apia
Muamua
'āiga everywhere
'Umu - 'ulu, taro, fa'i
rooster alarms
Gagana Sāmoa all around
loku, falesa, tatalo, pese

va'alele
first time
scared
all too new
windy cold air
fast angry cars
McDonalds, KFC, Fish n Chips

No English to All English
no friends to have as protectors.
only one 'āiga
on your own
Linden
Tawa
New Zealand

*Tenari Lieuteine, Year 9*

# Bad Blood

Let's start from the top.
Alofa is pure but it can also be fake,
hate is so strong
it's just take, take, take.
But wait, hold on supposed 'āiga!
Please ...
just give me a
break, break, break -
away to think if you are
blood or just related
tears flow like the blood your venom invaded.
Trying to penetrate this alofa with
your hatred.

So what's up with you?

Hate on us now because we are telling the truth
and we all know you can't handle to lose,
the game you are playing all by yourself
while you faikakala and smile
then deny me any help.
You're so nek level when you hide beside me,
pretend we are fine
with that fake twinkle in your eye.
But I hold back the words,
shaking my head
with a sigh,
because you need serious help, there's no need to lie.

It must be so hard
watching everyone's trust and alofa
walking out the door and out of your life.
Addicted to drama, not knowing the story
but making up more fables

while setting up toonai tables.
But if you were my blood,
you would know to stay true -
to us, the alofa, but more importantly to you.

Still we try to align
as blood we try to unite.
Yet you are blinded and can't see
it's like you were born to divide.
Love comes from the heart
to get to the heart,
Aren't you tired of hitting restart?
So why is there bad blood between us all?
How did this even become a silent war?
Can't help but think that there's a different door,
to bring us together not further apart.

But no one listens
no one's being smart.
We laugh, we giggle and jokes apply,
and the boiling bad blood we hide inside.
You don't need to worry,
I don't need to be sorry.
Let's just move on with all of His glory.
Please just ignore me,
but always remember,
I know what I know,
you cannot change any of it now
because at the end of the day
this is my story to tell.

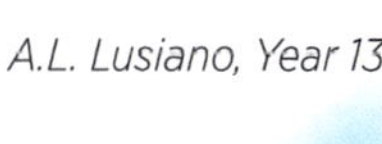

*A.L. Lusiano, Year 13*

# My Pasifika

Warming break of day
A beautiful ocean sings
Watching the palm trees

Rhythmic movement
Graceful siva, dancing, song
Move elegantly

Teaching our language
Proudly sharing gagana
Keeping it alive

Saying tatalo
Cultural Ta‘aloga
Fiafia nights

Fufulu ‘ipu
Fa‘amāmā le lapisi
Fai ou tiute

Singing and praying
Worshipping and fellowship
Charity and love

*Raelyn Viralolita Papalii, Year 7*

# Here and Whole

Dear 2020
Today marks the death of certainty,
it's the - rest now and got no activities later, or the rest of
this week it's the - "I'm here Sir" then turn off your camera
and mute the mic

Welcome to the year of stagnation

The elimination of conformity, routine and regularity

The cities deprived of human touch welcoming back natures hands
2020, You're forcing us to wrestle with our thoughts again,
To Evaluate, ponder, worry, and decipher,
to fear, to get anxious,
realise maybe now you have to care, to feel... again

It's the time of the month to deal with our demons
A time to adjust the focus and finally see in spectrums
we can let go of categories

No blue or pink, blend them, be purple, orange,
whatever you want,
you're at home right now anyways

This is our ode to the seas
Pulled by gravity
Compelled by forces alike
we are offspring of the tides
It's in our nature to crash against the rocks - sometimes

And still be standing Here and whole

Undamaged, unharmed, complete in mind soul and body
Proof that there is still salt in these veins

THIS is a sonnet to the Sun

That runs across the sky
A child of goodness
Kissing my melanin into deep darks illuminating dawns and dusks...
alleviating your struggles
And bbygal
with all THIS spare time
Its a chance to fix up those tan lines

THIS is for the year that was meant to be ours It's the breathe
before the jump

It is a tribute to the moon
And the bleeding hearts, adapting,

Discharging out the old and welcoming in the new

12 Months for 13 lunar phases,
the Moon always wanting to stay one step ahead
never showing its true face
It's when changes carry on WITH or WITHOUT you,
BUT i've been doing this for 17 years out of necessity

I've been glowing, beaming, flourishing

2016 i scoured my own heart
armed with nothing
and came out having taken back my crown

2018 i let my roots take form,
let them marvel in all its polycentricy,
curling back into pre colonial beauty

And this time of the year, i'll rest to complete the process

Continue to profess what i love about me

This endless transformation, this transgression of limitations

When time won't turn back

But lavish in the fact that this December will be different to the next, and the one after that

No matter how hard i'll ask for forgiveness, but not permission

To transition to a better version

I have this chance to build, to redesign, to restore, to revamp myself

To shed skin that doesn't fit my mold anymore

To reclaim
And be reborn again
If need be i'll fire upon it from ashes will rise new life

All this women, all this goodness, this ferocity,
this voluminous hair porosity, tenacious,
this audacity falling off the tip of my tongue

Here i am, complete

Sincerely:

The one that's still here and the one that's still whole

*Stellar Pritchard, Year 13*

*Breens Intermediate*
*Pasifika Group*

Harmony
Poly
Past
Family
Islands
Proud
Brown lives matter
Tokelauan
Elders
Thrive
Time
God
Rotuman
Samoan
Tongan
Family
Invisible
acceptance
connections
Respect
Serve
Pasifika
Fijian
Samoan
Connection
Kiribati
Culture
Solomon
Ancestors
Pray
Atua
Islander

# I am

Samoan.
Living a Samoan life at home
Samoan ‘ie lāvalava wearing, tulou saying,
a graceful chore cleaning servant.
Living a Pālagi life at school
speak my mind, opinion sharing, up against Pālagi headstarters.

30% Plastic
50% Samoan
20% Confused

loud, confident, social butterfly at school
quiet, cautious and graceful only at home
a true shape shifting tama‘ita‘i Sāmoa at heart

Samoan student
rising to Pālagi sunrises
returns to Sāmoa sunsets.
Constantly transforming between worlds
entering ‘social studies’ and leaving ‘Pacific studies.’

30% Plastic
50% Samoan
20% Transformer

white skinned Samoan speaking tama‘ita‘i
Samoan understanding Pālagi Samoan
Still a tama‘ita‘i Sāmoa
?

I am.

No matter how white my skin is.
No matter how Pālagi I dress.
No matter how many times I am asked.
No matter how you look at me.
No matter how, what, where, when and why ...

O a‘u o le tama‘ita‘i Sāmoa

0% Transformer
0% Plastic
0% Confused
100% Samoan

*Janet Vaiusu, Year 10*

# Taualuga

tapa wrapped
shallow breaths
beads dangle across my forehead
oil slathered arms
lipsticked cheeks

storytelling body movements
the history of my ancestors
honoured and privileged
eyes watching
following me with delight
elders relive their youth
from the crowd and up above

straighten my posture and smile
as if entering heaven
gates open
dignity overpowers my spirit
commanding respect
regal spotlight with softened fingers
gliding through the air
contagious alofa
excited spirits fill the room

grace embodied
true definition of a Teine Sāmoa.
family pride
blood over water
arms stretching out
courtesy and compassion
a nod, a smile

take a bow

*Mikaylah Teofilo, Year 8*

# A & B

**School A**

mentally & spiritually painful
for so many of us
class periods too long
drags on, gives teacher more
time
to talk, no teach
to hear their own voice.
10+ minutes for instructions
attention walks out the door
I wish I could go with it.
Content boring
sleep calling
whose interests are used for
learning?
They don't care about me
they're not interested in me
only focus on what I can't do
not what I can do.
Classes are too big
teachers can't manage
Some kids and their issues.
Can't handle and we know it
we can smell their fear and
stress.
Teachers don't know answers
or won't help me when I need
help
I need help.
Whole class punished because
of one student
not the islander team vibe
we need
making us part of the
consequences
feel like we are bad for
doing nothing
for being ourselves.
Uniform should be rewarded
with credits.
They're good at wasting time
being mini police
makes them more jaded.
This is why my friends are
important.
They make it fun
when no fun
is around.
Lifelong learning is with them
and not in this classroom.

**School B**

whanau vibes straight away
Caring staff
helpful when I needed it
even when I didn't need it.
Teachers were encouraging
uplifting to all the students
and were genuinely happy.
This made us students feel
happy.
Classes smaller and shorter
they got it right.
Content was broken down
into easy activities
my level of learning
learning made fun
didn't even know we were
learning.
Wanting to go to school
every day.
I knew I mattered
and my opinion was important.
I felt safe to say I didn't know
what the answer was
or how to do it
no feeling stupid or not worthy
to speak.

We didn't sit and read or write
all the time
always encouraged to move
around
lots of outdoor activities and
action based learning
laughter and genuine
enjoyment
made me want to finish tasks.
Walks to calm down
disruptive students were sent
out
so the class flow and energy was
not disrupted
dealt with straight away.
Uniforms did not turn into
behaviour issues,
Warehouse supplied shorts and
socks
plus school polo tops
easy, not expensive, no drama.
Some kids walked barefoot to
school
real marae style
tatou tatou vibes
not wanting 3 o'cock to come
and school life
all good.

*Brian Woolley, Year 12*

# Plastic

Pride in my identity and pride in my language
which i cannot speak.
Pride in my title -
PLASTIC
like the fake cow meat that makes up the pisupo
I ate with rice last night
PLASTIC
like the parts of the taxi my parents drive
PLASTIC
like the jolly drinks we drank at my cousin's party
PLASTIC
like the cheap packet of cheese and chicken flavoured bongo's
from super value
PLASTIC
like the one dollar bags of lollies from the dairy down
the street
PLASTIC
like the white knives from the takeaway shop that scratch
instead of cut
PLASTIC
like the tip top ice cream container that has to last
the whole week until payday
PLASTIC
like the glad wrap we use to wrap our mea'ai after to'ona'i
PLASTIC
like the bottles that litter our pacific oceans
and kills the creatures in it
PLASTIC
"Why can't you be like your cousin?"
PLASTIC
"Why you not speak Samoan?"
PLASTIC

Fobby accents are in, you are out
PLASTIC
Afraid to speak
PLASTIC
Don't want to look like an idiot
PLASTIC
Freeze, unable to respond
PLASTIC
"O are mai oe?"
"Manoo eya fay feet-tae"
PLASTIC
Frontin
living in the shadows
afraid of being
PLASTIC

*R.T., Year 9*

# Feaus

Feaus, oh feaus,
how I hate you feaus!

The pain you give my legs
going here and there
not some times -
All the time
Everywhere!

"Sau fai le ipu ti"
"Tapega le fale"
"Aumai la'u telefogi"

Do it again
and again
not for a short time
all of the time.
For the rest of my life time.
Moe, pray, clean.
Brings you closer to God.
The cleaner you are,
the cleaner your future.

Alu - Aumai - Fai - Kipi =
No faiga'elo here
there
or anywhere!

I am the Super Cleaner and Do-er!
Super feau power: service with a fake smile!
Super excited to salu the floor!
Pick up crumbs with my fingers!
And prays to God to give me a day off
... Maybe when I die.

*Mason Karini, Year 8*

# Grandad's Blue Eyed Taro Princess

It's an early Sunday morning.
I am a one year old.
I can smell the coconut cream goodness.
Bubbling away.

His shirt is ironed and tie is ready.
I see his suit jacket hanging.
The ‘ie lāvalava says Saoluafata, our village.
It's blue like the Pacific ocean.

Church ready, he returns to the stove.
The taro is drained.
Cut into pieces in my favourite pink bowl.
The cream is poured.

My little legs run to the table.
My plate appears.
It's breakfast time.
Off to church My Grandad goes.

Fast forward 10 years.
I am now eleven years old.
He now calls by phone.
"Your taro is ready."

In the car, on the way.
I smell the coconut cream.
I see him in his ‘ie faitaga ready for church.
A smile through the window greets me.

Quick hugs and steaming taro.
At the table he watches me savour every bite.
I smile back at him.
"Tall enough to do dishes now," he laughs.

More years have passed.
I peel the coarse brown skin.
Chopped up and in the pot.
Boiling away I look at My Grandad.

Is it as good as his?
He's too polite to say.
But made with love.
Like the love he has for me.
Grandad Selemaea's blue eyed taro princess.

*Amira Va'a, Year 7*

# Lost

**I**
a young female
Pacific Islander
live in an European country
**Am**
too plastic to be Samoan
too brown to be white
feeling excluded and exhausted
**Lost**
my language
who I am
knowing my roots, my ʻāiga
**Where**
standards are lowered
pitied on like my brownness disadvantages me
inequality walks in my shadow everyday
**Do**
something to step out of this white shadow
for me, for us to belong
not for us to be forgotten
**I**
am trying to find my place
want to grow brown roots
need a place to stand tall
**Belong?**
here, there or anywhere
to who and when
carrying forgotten Samoan legacies
this is who I am.

*Christina Taala, Year 11*

# Oku ‘iai ha kii fonua - The ocean of our land

I am a drop from the ocean of Tonga.
Kingdom of heaven on earth,
brown royalty.
Aho ‘eitu is a son of God
Siasi Uesiliana Tau’ataina ‘o Tonga.
Lotofale, lotu, himi.
Otua is everything.
Passed down
across ‘Oseni.

Great Grandma, Great Grandpa
first navigators, ancestors
vaka
to this fonua.
Drops of Tonga
Lea-faka.
Ngatu.
My culture, My heritage, My api,
My Soul.

“Ko e otua mo Tonga ko hoku tofia.”
“God and Tonga are my inheritance.”
Ko hingoa Siosifa ahau.
We are the ocean of our fonua
on your whenua.

*Joseph Koloa, Year 8*

KO E 'OTUA MO TONGA KO HOKU TOFI'A

# Tongues

Tongue of my Samoan ‘āiga
I once spoke fluently
passed down from ancestors.

Tongue of my tupuna
brown flames fight past the opening of my mouth
part of this knowledge is still clear.

Tongue of my Tokelauan ‘āiga
transitioned to new lands
starting over with new roots to be planted.

Tongue of my aunty's fale
new mother figure
giving me new life and learnings in this Pālagi world.

Tongue of my grandparents
I still hear to this day
brown moana waves forever echo in my ears
and crash against my hardened heart.

Tongue frozen

*Miliama Stephanie, Year 9*

# Whakapapa

Proclaiming my identity
when you don't know half of who you are?
Links to land and tribes
Real life survivor
the mana of those who came before
I feel.

Help me.

My whanau
Hauangi, Huri, Rangi, Moana and Mita.
my Samoan fanau
No one knows, not even me.
In the Maori class
fake
no language.

Imposter.

No connection to fathers homeland.
Don't even fit the stereotype
Just brown.
Like the dirt they feel beneath their feet.
Speeches start with kiaora
No tālofa in sight
Like the plastic flowers sold in dollar stores.

I whakapapa back to tikanga and broken promises.

Disconnected from my family tree
starving to be whole in the eyes of Atua who brought me here
Searching for my place In this world
Praying
Pleading
Begging

Whakapapa
Whakapapa

I'm here
Find me.

*Maria Kauri Seulu, Year 8*

# Choices

The route was clear
instructions were;
to turn right,
but never look left.
So I follow their rules
until I got to a point.
Right there, I knew.

This certain road paved for me,
Does not align with my destination.
What is this thing, destiny?
Spirits whisper,
it is located to my left,
but
that's where everything is left behind
swallowed by the sea
told to me by the world
that place -
it is not meant for me.

Last two steps.
Hawks watching my every move.
I have to be careful,
I hear them talking,
I see them lurking.
Right around the corner,
but the moana is calling
to risk it all,
journey beyond the path laid out
look to my left
make it your last step.

The moana
is where the sun begins and ends,
how can the left not be for me
or my friends?
Dispel all the myths,
see heads peeking,
tongues ready to lash out.

At a crossroads
I don't know what to do.
So here I am.
Stuck with choices -
Which way to go?
Left or right?

Who and when to be?

*Fetu Iosia, Year 13*

fa'afetai lava,
mālo 'aupito,
fakaaue lahi,
meitaki maata,
fakafetai,
tenkyu tenkyu tru tenkyu tumas,
vinaka,
ko raba,
fakafetai lasi,
ngā mihi nui.

I remember the first time I met Joy Cowley, one of New Zealand's most prolific and successful writers of children's books. Our talanoa centred around the need for Māori and Pasifika stories for our tamaiti whom we both agreed have been missing from the pages of the stories they read. I excitedly told Joy about the Pasifika Navigators book project and the idea of helping our tamaiti to reconnect with their storytelling spirits. Like little children, we dreamed with our eyes open about the endless possibilities of all our Pasifika and Māori tamaiti finally being able to be seen, heard, and valued as themselves. At the end of our story sharing and dream exchanging talanoa, Joy turned to me and said something I will never forget - "Dahlia, your stories bring your people home."

This made me think of home. Our roots as Pasifika and where we have come from to where we are now. From personal experience I have learnt that great navigation skills are needed to problem solve, manage, and balance the worlds we live in, especially when our search for belonging and acceptance has always included a series of cultural challenges and choices. So like most Mila's Books projects, I took a deep breath, a pocket full of prayers and in one school term, through in person and online workshops, countless feedback emails and ongoing communication with a mixture of reluctant writers, first time poets and passionate writers, we gathered a collection of Pasifika hearts and souls on paper. Voices that have been waiting to be unleashed. Words that mirrored many of our thoughts and feelings as Pasifika here in Aotearoa. And my favourite part, proud Pasifika tamaiti feeling empowered to be themselves.

So many amazing people made this book possible, ensuring that our va'a was secured and strengthened by faith, tautua and alofa along the way. Gabby Makisi and Opal Soutar from the Ministry of Education enabled the winds that launched this va'a into the great moana nui a kiwa. For your belief and trust in us at Mila's Books to do what has never been done before and for supporting us to create a much needed space for our tamaiti to share their thoughts, experiences and learnings the Pasifika way - fa'afetai tele lava from the bottom of our hearts.

We acknowledge those who encouraged our navigators to explore, question and reflect, leading them to new ways of better connecting with each other on their life long journeys. These are the amazing educators who supported this book project from the beginning - Katie Rawles (Tawa College), Catherine Ryan (Bishop Viard College), Samuel Tanielu (St Pauls College), Leki Jackson-Bourke (Marcellin College), Amy Moli and Marion Iosefo (Hastings Girls High School), Sinapi Taeao (Naenae College), Nathaniel Maclennan and Stephanie Pole (Breens Intermediate School), Komia Va'a (Wainuiomata Intermediate School), Sam Winnie (Naenae Intermediate School) and the parents/caregivers of individual contributors who submitted poems outside of the school groups I had the honour to work with. Fa'afetai tele lava to you all for seeing the potential in this book project and using it as an opportunity to show the world and our tamaiti the Pasifika storytelling powers they possess.

Finally, to our contributing navigators, who stepped aboard our storytelling va'a, we thank you. Not just for your time, energy, and commitment to the project, but for the amazing talanoa, the laughs and tears along the way. For being nothing but yourself while sharing your lessons and heartfelt messages with the world. Always remember you are enough, and like our ancestors you are true navigators and storytellers whose words have the power to inspire, change the world, and most importantly, bring our people home.

Manuia lou malaga,
Dahlia Malaeulu
*Mila's Books Publisher*

## Calling all Pasifika Navigators!

**Contact us at www.milasbooks.com if you or your school are interested in submitting poetry, short stories or a piece of writing to be considered for future Pasifika Navigators publications.**

## TE MOANA-NUI-A-KIWA POETS

During one of our writing workshops a student said, "This poetry thing is pretty cool ... Do we have islander poets Miss? We don't really learn about them at school, I wish we did. Maybe we can include a list of poets in the book for all of us navigators and our teachers?" Here is who they came up with:

Karlo Mila

Mere Taito

Courtney Sina Meredith

Sia Figiel

Selina Tusitala Marsh

Doug Poole

Tusiata Avia

Serie Barford

Grace Teuila Taylor

Albert Wendt

Audrey Brown-Pereira

Reverend Mua Strickson-Pua

Leilani Tamu

Simone Kaho

Audrey Brown-Pereira

Momoe Malietoa Von Reiche

Nafanua PK

Nicky Perese

Haunani-Kay Trask

Niusila Faamantu-Eteuati

Sisilia Eteuati

Ria Masae

Rebecca Tobo Olul-Hosen

Daisy Lavea-Timo

Lastman Sooula

Aigagalefili Fepulea'i

Tapua'i Teresia Teaiwa

Daren Kamali

Keri Hulme

Vau Peseta

John Puhiatau Pule

Penina Ava Taesali

Konai Helu Thaman

Alistair Te Ariki Campbell

Sina Va'ai

Apisai Enos Papua

John Dominis Holt

Imaikalani Kalahele

Kathy Jetnil-Kijiner

Peter Onedera

Caroline Sinavaiana-Gabbard

Lehua M. Taitano

Grace Teuila Taylor

Wayne Kaumualii Westlake

Kauraka Kauraka

Jully Makini

Dan Taulapapa McMullin

Grace Mera Molisa

Craig Santos Perez

Steven Edmund Winduo

Faith Wilson
(Saufo'i Press - Publisher of
Moana Pacific poetry books)

## Mila's Books

We create books that help Pasifika to be seen, heard and valued through the power of our stories.

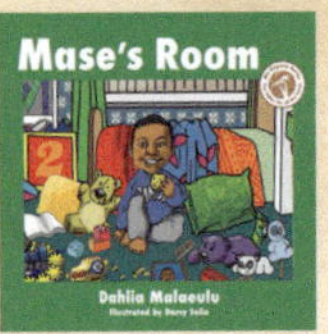


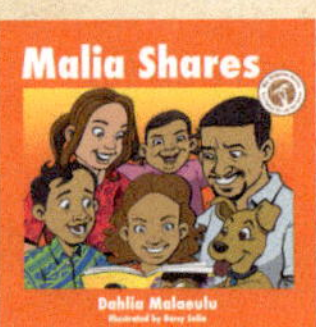


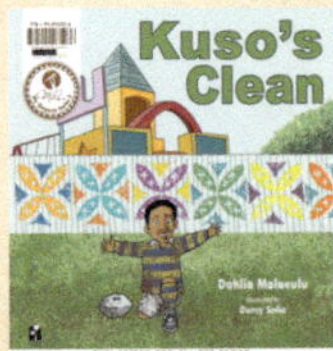

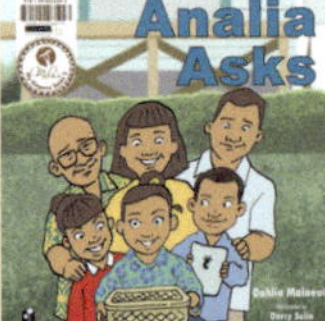


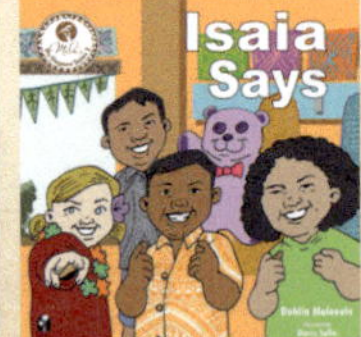


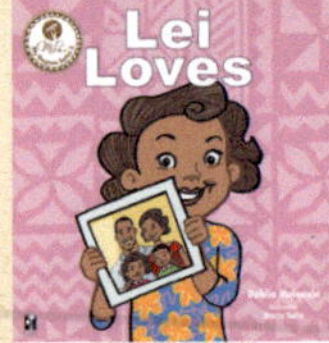

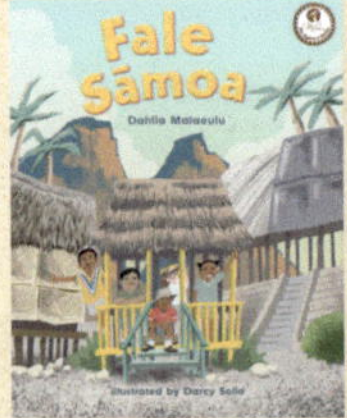


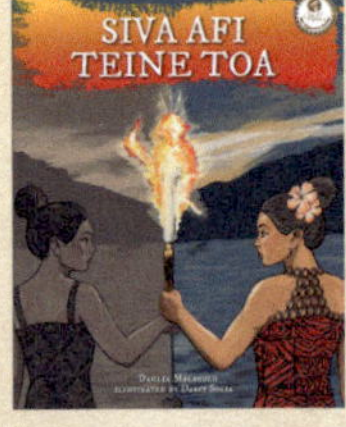

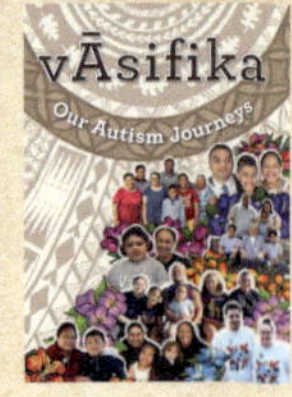